# 5-Fold
# Leadership

*...in the marketplace*

*Harold Herring*

www.HaroldHerring.com

Debt Free Army
PO Box 900000, Fort Worth, TX 76161

5–Fold Leadership in the Marketplace
by Harold Herring

ISBN: 978-0-9763668-6-7
Copyright © 2015 by the Debt Free Army
PO Box 900000, Fort Worth, TX 76161
817-222-0011
harold@haroldherring.com

Unless otherwise noted, Scripture references are taken
from the King James Version of the Bible.

# 5-Fold Leadership
## ...in the marketplace

*Including these God-Given Topics:*

# All ... Includes You

When it comes to fulfilling available leadership positions ... it's always important to know if you possess all the qualifications necessary for consideration.

> The keys to unlock great wisdom, ability and expertise are found only in His presence.

Let's look at all your scriptural qualifications.

Exodus 31:3 in the New Living Translation says:

*"I have filled him with the Spirit of God, giving him great wisdom, ability, and expertise in all kinds of crafts."*

Where does "great wisdom, ability and expertise" come from? The Spirit of God.

Who does the Spirit of God give "great wisdom, ability and expertise" to?

To all God's children, and that includes you.

1 Corinthians 12:4-7 in the Amplified Bible says:

> *"Now there are distinctive varieties and distributions of endowments (gifts, extraordinary powers distinguishing certain Christians, due to the power of divine grace operating in their souls by the Holy Spirit) and they vary, but the [Holy] Spirit remains the same."* *(Verse 4)*

There are "gifts and extraordinary powers" available to you through the power of the Holy Spirit.

> *"And there are distinctive varieties of service and ministration, but it is the same Lord [Who is served].*
>
> *"And there are distinctive varieties of operation [of working to accomplish things], but it is the same God Who inspires and energizes them all in all."* *(Verses 5-6)*

Did you notice the scripture says that God "inspires and energizes them all in all"?

> When the scripture says "all," does that include you?

You are included in "all."

> *"But to each one is given the manifestation of the [Holy] Spirit [the evidence, the spiritual illumination of the Spirit] for good and profit."* *(Verse 7)*

God is giving gifts and extraordinary powers to ALL His children whom He will inspire and energize so we can achieve our destiny for good and profit.

God is working with you ... in all things ... at all times.

Romans 8:28 says:

> *"And we know that all things work together for good to them that love God, to them who are the called according to his purpose."*

Now let's look at the Amplified Bible translation of Romans 8:28 which says:

> *"We are assured and know that [God being a partner in their labor] all things work together and are [fitting into a plan] for good to and for those who love God and are called according to [His] design and purpose."*

The only criteria in all things working together for your success is whether or not you love God and are called according to His purpose.

Do you love God? That's an easy ... *yes* or *no* ... question.

Are you called according to His purpose?

Before answering that ... let me ask you one other question. Is this question specifically directed to any group of people? Does the verse say that this question is for people who are called to traditional full-time church ministry positions? No, of course not.

This question isn't limited to those who work in the four walls of a church building.

All means everybody, and that includes you.

> The wisdom of the world says that all good things come to those who wait. The Word of God says that all things come now.

2 Corinthians 9:8 in the Amplified Bible says:

> *"And God is able to make **all** grace (every favor and earthly blessing) come to you in abundance, so that you may always and under **all** circumstances and whatever the need be self-sufficient [possessing enough to require no aid or support and furnished in abundance for every good work and charitable donation]."*

You're to get all God's grace ... translated as "every favor and earthly blessing" in abundance so that in all circumstances you don't require any support but rather you're supporting other people.

Once again, is this verse just for those who have a master's or doctorate in theology ... pastor the largest church in the city ... or have been on the mission field for twenty years? Of course not.

Once again ... all means everybody, and you are included in everybody.

Are there limitations to what you can do? Not according to Philippians 4:13 which says:

> *"I can do all things through Christ which strengtheneth me."*

The Greek word for "all things" is *pas* (G3956) and it means:

**"each, every, any, all, the whole, everyone, all things, everything."**

I'd say that according to the Word of God "all things" means without limitation.

God will not hold anything back ... He will give us all things.

Romans 8:32 in the Amplified Bible says:

> "He who did not withhold or spare [even] His own Son but gave Him up for us all, will He not also with Him freely and graciously give us all [other] things?"

Is there a key to us receiving "all things"?

Absolutely! It's found in Matthew 28:20:

> "Teaching them to observe everything that I have commanded you, and behold, I am with you all the days (perpetually, uniformly, and on every occasion), to the [very] close and consummation of the age. Amen (so let it be)."

When we do all that He says ... then He will bless us in all things.

Matthew 6:33 says:

> "But seek ye first the kingdom of God, and his righteousness; and all these things shall be added unto you."

The Contemporary English Version of Matthew 6:33 says:

> "But more than anything else, put God's work first and do what he wants. Then the other things will be yours as well."

At the same time that you're increasing your effectiveness in ministry and/or business God will be increasing your authority over all the things in planet earth.

Hebrews 2:8 in the New Living Translation says:

*"You gave them authority over all things."*

Now when it says "all things," it means nothing is left out. But we have not yet seen all things put under their authority.

Are you wondering if money is included in all things?

Absolutely! Consider the words of Ecclesiastes 10:19:

*"A feast is made for laughter, and wine maketh merry: but money answereth all things."*

The manifestation of His all in and through your life … is not based on your education, who your parents are or anything else. It's simply by believing the Word.

In Matthew 21:22 the scripture says:

*"And all things, whatsoever ye shall ask in prayer, believing, ye shall receive."*

If you've gotten this teaching now inside of you … we can continue to the next chapter … if not, please read it again.

# The 7 Characteristics
# of a Priest

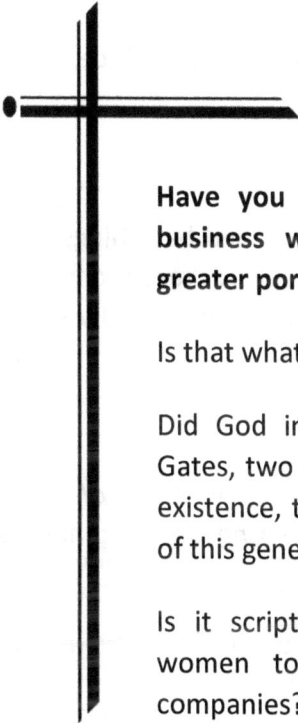

**Have you ever wondered why the secular business world seems to flourish but the greater portion of God's Kingdom lags behind?**

Is that what God intended?

Did God intend for Warren Buffett and Bill Gates, two men who have questioned His very existence, to be considered the financial gurus of this generation?

Is it scripturally wrong for Godly men and women to found and direct Fortune 500 companies?

**Did God design the business world to be separate from the church?**

First, let's establish the fact that there's very clear distinction made in the scripture between a king and a priest.

Revelation 1:6 says:

> *"And hath made us kings and priests unto God and his Father; to him be glory and dominion for ever and ever. Amen."*

In Israel, it's very clear from the scriptures that kings and priests held two very distinct and different offices.

Here are seven things that characterize the office of the priest.

## 1. Hearing from God

The priest would hear good things and bad things as it related to the children of Israel ... based on their behavior and how they followed or didn't follow God's instructions.

Hosea 5:1 says:

> *"Hear ye this, O priests; and hearken, ye house of Israel; and give ye ear, O house of the king; for judgment is toward you ..."*

When the priest didn't hear the Word of God it was because he was tolerating sin in his life.

## 2. Receiving Tithes and Offerings

Hebrews 7:5-6 in the Amplified Bible says:

> *"And it is true that those descendants of Levi who are charged with the priestly office are commanded in the Law to take tithes from the people—which means, from*

their brethren—though these have descended from Abraham.*"

## 3. Offering Sacrifices for the People

Leviticus 1:5-9 in the Amplified Bible paints a vivid picture of the priests' responsibility in helping the people.

*"The man shall kill the young bull before the Lord, and the priests, Aaron's sons, shall present the blood and dash [it] round about upon the altar that is at the door of the Tent of Meeting.*

*"And he shall skin the burnt offering and cut it into pieces. And the sons of Aaron the priest shall put fire on the altar and lay wood in order on the fire; And Aaron's sons the priests shall lay the pieces, the head and the fat, in order on the wood on the fire on the altar.*

*"But its entrails and its legs he shall wash with water. And the priest shall burn all of it on the altar for a burnt offering, an offering by fire, a sweet and satisfying odor to the Lord."*

## 4. Rallying the People for Battles

2 Chronicles 13:14-16 in the Message Bible says:

*"They prayed desperately to God, the priests blew their trumpets, and the soldiers of Judah shouted their battle cry. At the battle cry, God routed Jeroboam and all Israel before Abijah and Judah. The army of Israel scattered before Judah; God gave them the victory ..."*

## 5. Attending to the Needs of the Widows and Orphans

Deuteronomy 26:13 in the New Living Translation says:

*"Then you must declare in the presence of the Lord your God, 'I have taken the sacred gift from my house and have given it to the Levites, foreigners, orphans, and widows, just as you commanded me. I have not violated or forgotten any of your commands.' "*

## 6. Caring for the House of God

According to Numbers 3:38 in the New International Version ... Aaron and his sons *"... were responsible for the care of the sanctuary on behalf of the Israelites ..."*

Numbers 18:3 says:

*"And they shall keep thy charge, and the charge of all the tabernacle ..."*

## 7. Preventing Strangers from Entering the Temple

This final characteristic goes one step further than the priests just caring for the sanctuary ... they were to protect it ... even with lethal force ... against strangers.

Numbers 3:38 says:

*"... and the stranger that cometh nigh shall be put to death."*

The stranger could be someone from a foreign land or it could be someone who did not believe. Even those who did believe in our great God Jehovah were not allowed to enter.

If a stranger was allow to enter ... it was not just trouble for the priest but for the entire nation.

Numbers 18:4-5 in the Amplified Bible says:

"... and no stranger [no layman, anyone who is not a Levite] shall come near you [Aaron and your sons].

"And you shall attend to the duties of the sanctuary and attend to the altar [of burnt offering and the altar of incense], that there be no wrath any more upon the Israelites."

The priest is to provide the vision for his people and any others who wander by.

# The 7 Characteristics of a King

Now let's look at the seven things that characterize the office of the king.

## 1. Honoring God as the Ultimate Authority of the Nation

Psalm 63:11 in the Amplified Bible says:

*"But the king shall rejoice in God; everyone who swears by Him [that is, who binds himself by God's authority, acknowledging His supremacy, and devoting himself to His glory and service alone; every such one] shall glory, for the mouths of those who speak lies shall be stopped."*

## 2. Governing the Affairs of the People

Ecclesiastes 8:4 in the Amplified Bible says:

*"For the word of a king is authority and power, and who can say to him, What are you doing?"*

### 3. Protecting the Nation Against Attacks of Their Enemies

1 Samuel 8:20 in the Amplified Bible says:

*"That we also may be like all the nations, and that our king may govern us and go out before us and fight our battles."*

### 4. Providing Tithes and Offerings to the Priests

2 Chronicles 24:11 in the New Living Translation says:

*"Whenever the chest became full, the Levites would carry it to the king's officials. Then the court secretary and an officer of the high priest would come and empty the chest and take it back to the Temple again. This went on day after day, and a large amount of money was collected."*

### 5. Collecting the Spoils of War

Hebrews 7:1 in The Message Bible says:

*"[Melchizedek, Priest of God] Melchizedek was king of Salem and priest of the Highest God. He met Abraham, who was returning from 'the royal massacre,' and gave him his blessing. Abraham in turn gave him a tenth of the spoils. 'Melchizedek' means 'King of Righteousness.' 'Salem' means 'Peace.' So, he is also 'King of Peace.' Melchizedek towers out of the past—without record of family ties, no account of beginning or end. In this way he is like the Son of God, one huge priestly presence dominating the landscape always."*

## 6. Obeying the Instructions and Direction of God

2 Kings 23:1-3 in Today's New International Version says:

*"When the king called together all the elders of Judah and Jerusalem. He went up to the temple of the LORD with the people of Judah, the inhabitants of Jerusalem, the priests and the prophets—all the people from the least to the greatest. He read in their hearing all the words of the Book of the Covenant, which had been found in the temple of the LORD. The king stood by the pillar and renewed the covenant in the presence of the LORD—to follow the LORD and keep his commands, statutes and decrees with all his heart and all his soul, thus confirming the words of the covenant written in this book. Then all the people pledged themselves to the covenant."*

## 7. Settling Disputes Among His People

2 Samuel 15:2 in the Amplified Bible says:

*"And [he] rose up early and stood beside the gateway; and when any man who had a controversy came to the king for judgment, Absalom called to him, Of what city are you? And he would say, Your servant is of such and such a tribe of Israel."*

So, fundamentally, there is a priestly and a kingly anointing, and they're available to you.

# Do These Gifts Apply to You?

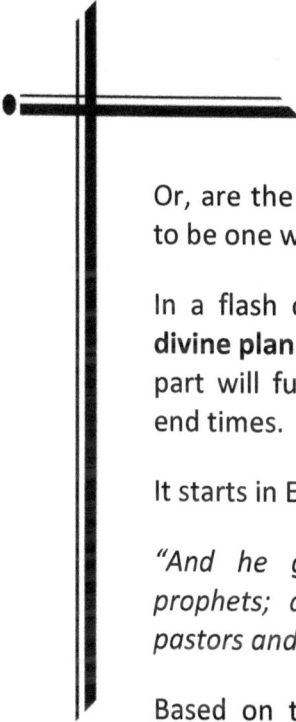

Or, are the world and God's kingdom designed to be one with each other?

In a flash of revelation, **God showed me His divine plan for mankind.** What we have seen in part will fully come together as we enter the end times.

It starts in Ephesians 4:11:

*"And he gave some, apostles; and some, prophets; and some, evangelists; and some, pastors and teachers."*

Based on the viewpoints of many Christians, they feel this verse should probably say:

*"And he gave some, apostles (from Rhema Bible Training Center); and some, prophets (from Christ For The Nations Institute); and some, evangelists (from Southeastern Baptist Seminary); and some, pastors (from Lee College) and teachers (from Oral Roberts University)."*

The five offices mentioned in Ephesians 4:11 are not restricted to those who've had religious training nor are they limited to the four walls of a church.

Although we are accustomed to looking at Ephesians 4:11 from the dimension of the Christian ministry, I soon discovered these gifts and callings have always been God's plan for His global reach for the Kingdom.

Yes, Ephesians 4:11 talks about ministry offices ... but it's so much more than that.

**You have a calling you qualify for ... He wants you to recognize and walk in that calling.**

Let's look a little closer at these offices ... even though you may have never felt called into the ministry as we traditionally interpret the call of God.

# Are You an Apostle?

Don't dismiss my question out of hand … without fully considering what the scripture has to say about being an apostle … in ministry or in the marketplace.

**First, let's look at the Apostle.**

The word *apostle* is the Greek word *apostolos* (G652) and it's found entirely in the New Testament.

*Apostolos* is found 81 times in 80 verses in the Greek Concordance of the King James Version of the Bible.

In 19 of those verses it's the singular word *apostle* which is defined as:

**"a delegate, messenger, one sent forth with orders."**

This definition has always been applied to a religious delegate or messenger.

I would submit to you ... **that if God has given you or any other believer a vision ... a dream ... a passion ... a direction ... an instruction to start your own business ...** then you are a "delegate," "messenger" or "one sent forth with orders."

The apostle is the head of an organization ... whether a ministry or business.

An apostle can start something out of nothing ... has the ability to bring people together in a group for a specific purpose ... the ability to mentor and develop people into leaders by developing specific skill sets.

**The apostle sees, understands and develops the big picture ... the business plan.** The apostle also, out of vision and necessity, has the ability to function in any of the other ministry/business offices. That's what makes the apostle a great mentor.

**The apostle is the leader ... separated from others to form a business ... to lead.** Romans 1:1 in the Message Bible says:

> *"I, Paul, am a devoted slave of Jesus Christ on assignment, authorized as an apostle to proclaim God's words and acts. I write this letter to all the believers in Rome, God's friends."*

**Proclaiming God's words and acts is more than just the traditional interpretation of preaching the gospel.**

God's word tells every believer how to be successful ... whether in business or ministry. I could give you dozens of scriptures to emphasize this point ... but I'm just going to give you four.

Joshua 1:8 tells us:

> *"This book of the law shall not depart out of thy mouth; but thou shalt meditate therein day and night, that thou mayest observe to do according to all that is written therein: for then thou shalt make thy way prosperous, and then thou shalt have good success."*

Ephesians 3:20 in the New Living Translation says:

> *"Now all glory to God, who is able, through his mighty power at work within us, to accomplish infinitely more than we might ask or think."*

2 Thessalonians 1:11 in the New Living Translation says:

> *"So we keep on praying for you, asking our God to enable you to live a life worthy of his call. May he give you the power to accomplish all the good things your faith prompts you to do."*

Mark 9:23 in the GOD'S WORD Translation tells us:

> *"Jesus said to him, 'As far as possibilities go, everything is possible for the person who believes.' "*

The apostle according to Romans 11:13 in the Contemporary English Version of the Bible takes pride in his/her work.

> *"I am now speaking to you Gentiles, and as long as I am an apostle to you, I will take pride in my work."*

The Amplified Bible translation of Romans 11:13 says the Apostle magnifies the office.

An Apostle is called through the will of God. 1 Corinthians 1:1 says:

> *"Paul called to be an apostle of Jesus Christ through the will of God, and Sosthenes our brother."*

I believe God calls people into business for His purpose … just as He does into ministry for His purpose.

2 Corinthians 12:12 in the Amplified Bible says:

> *"Indeed, the signs that indicate a [genuine] apostle were performed among you fully and most patiently in miracles and wonders and mighty works."*

The apostle is an effective communicator … **encouraging those who are involved with him/her in ministry and/or business.**

Ephesians 1:1 in the Amplified Bible says:

> *"Paul, an apostle (special messenger) of Christ Jesus (the Messiah), by the divine will (the purpose and the choice of God) to the saints (the consecrated, set-apart ones) at Ephesus who are also faithful and loyal and steadfast in Christ Jesus."*

Apostles whether in ministry or business should always be truthful and filled with faith about the vision God gave them to fulfill.

1 Timothy 2:7 in the Contemporary English Version of the Bible says:

> *"This is why God chose me to be a preacher and an apostle of the good news. I am telling the truth. I am not*

*lying. God sent me to teach the Gentiles about faith and truth."*

**One of the major functions of apostles in the church is to duplicate themselves by discipling and raising up other leaders.** That's also the function of the apostle in the marketplace.

2 Kings 2:9 in the New Living Translation says:

> *"When they came to the other side, Elijah said to Elisha, 'Tell me what I can do for you before I am taken away.' And Elisha replied, 'Please let me inherit a double share of your spirit and become your successor.' "*

Successful apostles ... regardless of their vocation ... make it their business to find, mentor and train people to maintain and expand their vision. **A vision from God is never meant to die.**

In the business environment there is a chain of command ... a corporate ladder to climb ... a proving of yourself to be worthy of the opportunity ... the calling to assume the mantle of the apostle ... the Chief Executive Officer (CEO) or President of the company.

God may not have called you to be an apostle in the traditional sense of ministry, but the marketplace is a far more fertile field for ministry than the four walls of a church could ever be.

# Are You a Prophet?

**Second, let's look at the Prophet.**

The Greek word for *prophet* found in Ephesians 4:11 is *prophētēs* (G4396) and it means:

> **"one moved by the spirit who speaks forth; they discerned and did what is best for the Christian cause, foretelling certain future events."**

The Greek for *prophet* comes from two root words which literally mean:

> **"to make known one's thoughts before."**

Prophets have three distinct characteristics.

## 1. The prophet is able to forecast or predict the future.

Acts 11:27-28 in the Amplified Bible says:

*"And during these days prophets (inspired teachers and interpreters of the divine will and purpose) came down*

from Jerusalem to Antioch. And one of them named Agabus stood up and prophesied through the [Holy] Spirit that a great and severe famine would come upon the whole world. And this did occur during the reign of Claudius."

## 2. The prophet offers direction for the future.

Acts 13:1-3 in the New Living Translation says:

"Among the prophets and teachers of the church at Antioch of Syria were Barnabas, Simeon (called 'the black man'), Lucius (from Cyrene), Manaen (the childhood companion of King Herod Antipas), and Saul. One day as these men were worshiping the Lord and fasting, the Holy Spirit said, 'Dedicate Barnabas and Saul for the special work to which I have called them.' So after more fasting and prayer, the men laid their hands on them and sent them on their way."

## 3. The prophet monitors situations and offers correction as needed.

Acts 15:32 in the Amplified Bible says:

"And Judas and Silas, who were themselves prophets (inspired interpreters of the will and purposes of God), urged and warned and consoled and encouraged the brethren with many words and strengthened them."

In short, **the prophet is able to forecast the future, offer suggestions for direction and provide correction as needed**.

In the natural realm, I've just described the CFO (Chief

Financial Officer) or COO (Chief Operating Officer) of a business.

If you want to run a successful business, either corporate or home-based … this gift is essential to your financial stability and future.

**The words of the prophet must be time-tested and proven true.**

Acts 11:28 in the Amplified Bible says:

> *"And one of them named Agabus stood up and prophesied through the [Holy] Spirit that a great and severe famine would come upon the whole world. And this did occur during the reign of Claudius."*

**The value of any CFO/COO must be weighed by the accuracy of their projections.**

Oftentimes, the words of the prophet (CFO/COO) must be reviewed and verified by outside firms.

1 Corinthians 14:29 says:

> *"Let the prophets speak two or three, and let the other judge."*

**The CFO/COO must work closely with the CEO just as the apostle and prophet work closely together.**

Ephesians 2:20 says:

> *"And are built upon the foundation of the apostles and prophets, Jesus Christ himself being the chief corner stone."*

# Are You an Evangelist?

**Third, let's look at the Evangelist.**

The Greek word for *evangelist* is *euaggelistēs* (G2099) and is defined as:

> **"to bring good news, to announce glad tidings."**

The purpose of an evangelist is to spread the Good News, to increase the number of recruits (converts).

In the business world ... this would be the function of a Vice-President or Director of Sales. Good salespeople are honest and focused on their assignment.

A great example of a salesman is found in the life of Philip in Acts 6:3-7 in the Amplified Bible.

In Verse 3 ... we see that **salespeople are chosen because of their good character and reputation.** A good salesman is also **knowledgeable about his product.**

*"Therefore select out from among yourselves, brethren, seven men of good and attested character and repute, full of the [Holy] Spirit and wisdom, whom we may assign to look after this business and duty."*

In Verse 4 ... we read where **the salesman is always involved in continuing education and mentorship.**

*"But we will continue to devote ourselves steadfastly to prayer and the ministry of the Word."*

In Verse 5 ... we see where a good salesperson is **confident about his/her product and/or service.**

*"And the suggestion pleased the whole assembly, and they selected Stephen, a man full of faith (a strong and welcome belief that Jesus is the Messiah) and full of and controlled by the Holy Spirit, and Philip ... **(and a bunch of other folks)."***

In Verse 6 ... good salespeople **learn everything they can from more experienced salespeople ... those who've paid the price and learned the ropes.**

*"These they presented to the apostles, who after prayer laid their hands on them."*

In Verse 7 ... we read **where good salespeople produce great results ... expanding their territory and increasing the number of customers.**

*"And the message of God kept on spreading, and the number of disciples multiplied greatly in Jerusalem; and [besides] a large number of the priests were obedient to the faith [in Jesus as the Messiah, through Whom is*

*obtained eternal salvation in the kingdom of God]."*

One final reference ... good salespeople know they will **experience some rejection in order to achieve their ultimate goal.**

2 Timothy 4:5 in the Contemporary English Version says:

*"But you must stay calm and be willing to suffer. You must work hard to tell the good news and to do your job well."*

# Are You a Pastor?

**Fourth, let's look at the Pastor.**

The Greek word for *pastor* is *poimēn* (G4166) and is defined as:

**"he to whose care and control others have committed themselves, and whose precepts they follow."**

The Greek word for *pastor* appears 18 times in 17 verses according to the Greek Concordance of the King James Bible.

It's interesting to note that in 15 of those 18 times pastor is mentioned … the word for *pastor* is translated as *shepherd*.

In reading those 15 references … in most instances, the scripture is talking about the shepherd protecting his flock … or his folks from harm. He is caring for them and leading them to safety. He/she wants to make sure they're blessed and not walking into harm's way.

In the marketplace, **the pastor would be the Vice-President of Customer Relations.** I want you to bear this in mind as we review what I consider to be the best job description and example of a pastor/shepherd/elder found in scripture.

1 Peter 5:1-4 in the Amplified Bible says:

> *"I warn and counsel the elders among you (the pastors and spiritual guides of the church) as a fellow elder and as an eyewitness [called to testify] of the sufferings of Christ, as well as a sharer in the glory (the honor and splendor) that is to be revealed (disclosed, unfolded):*

> *"Tend (nurture, guard, guide, and fold) the flock of God that is [your responsibility], not by coercion or constraint, but willingly; not dishonorably motivated by the advantages and profits [belonging to the office], but eagerly and cheerfully."*

A good Customer Relations Director will maintain a proper balance between protecting the interests of his employer with the best interests of the customer/consumer the company serves.

Verse 3 ... points out that **the Customer Relations personnel should treat everyone the way they want to be treated ... with respect.**

> *"Not domineering [as arrogant, dictatorial, and over-bearing persons] over those in your charge, but being examples (patterns and models of Christian living) to the flock (the congregation).*

> *"And [then] when the Chief Shepherd is revealed, you will win the conqueror's crown of glory."*

When it comes time for promotions ... the Customer Relations Director who has done the best job ... will receive the greatest reward.

# Are You a Teacher?

**Fifth and finally, let's look at the Teacher.**

The Greek word for *teacher* is *didaskalos* (G1320) and it's defined as:

> **"one who teaches concerning the things of God, and the duties of man; one who is fitted to teach, or thinks himself so."**

The teacher brings instruction to the Body of Christ. **The teacher is there to help equip the church so they can enjoy a fruitful, productive life … one worth living.**

In the marketplace, the teacher would be the Director of Training or perhaps the Vice-President of Human Relations.

The qualities of the teacher are best described in Colossians 3:16 in the Amplified Bible:

> *"Let the word [spoken by] Christ (the Messiah) have its home [In your hearts and minds] and dwell in you in [all*

*its] richness, as you teach and admonish and train one another in all insight and intelligence and wisdom [in spiritual things, and as you sing] psalms and hymns and spiritual songs, making melody to God with [His] grace in your hearts."*

**Every teacher wants the words of information and instruction they speak to become rooted and grounded in their students.**

When instruction from the Word of God is followed, the student enjoys a better quality of life and a higher degree of contentment within their profession.

A teacher's job is to prepare the next generation to carry on the work of the ministry and/or the business to ensure further growth, development and outreach.

**One final note. For way too long …** way too many believers have felt the only way they could be of service to the Kingdom of God was by operating in the 5-fold ministry within the church.

I believe both the Kings and the Priests operate in the 5-fold ministry.

**The Priest provides the vision from God and the King responds with the provision.**

It's time to expand our thought processes and ask God to stir up creative, economically profitable ideas … so we can begin operating in the end-time office of the Giver.

Do you want to start your own business?

Have you read secular books on developing a proper business plan?

Are you wondering how to compete in the marketplace?

Have you attended a high-priced seminar to gain instructions on the proper business techniques?

Have you sought the advice of others on the organizational structure of a successful enterprise?

Do you realize that God has designed a business structure for the perilous times that we're living in?

# A Final Thought About Your Leadership

I'd like for you to read this scripture again.

Ephesians 4:11 says:

*"And he gave some, apostles; and some, prophets; and some, evangelists; and some, pastors and teachers."*

I feel prompted to ask you several more questions about that verse.

**Does the scripture call the five offices listed "the 5-fold ministry"?**

Would it surprise you to know that the term "5-fold ministry" is not in the King James Version of the Bible or any of the other 13 translations that I searched?

The term "5-fold ministry" is a term coined by leaders in the church.

<u>Does it say in Ephesians 4:11 that those offices function only</u>

in the four walls of a local church or in religious/ministry settings around the world?

I heard Dr. Morris Cerullo say years ago that all truth is parallel. It would appear that **God did not restrict Ephesians 4:11 to just ministry but has given us a sound business platform as well as a ministry platform.**

We should be seeing a lot more of these principles played out in the days ahead.

# 7 Leadership Keys
# for Your Vision

In Proverbs 29:18 King Solomon said:

*"Where there is no vision, the people perish: but he that keepeth the law, happy is he."*

According to Strong's Concordance the Hebrew word for *vision* is *chazown* (H2377) which means:

> **"vision, oracle, prophecy (divine communication)."**

This literally means a revelatory unction and direction from the Lord.

**When you have a vision, it's personal ... it's unique to you ... something that's God ordained and visualized to be a part of your life**. That's why a vision is different from a goal.

Your goals will flow out of your vision. <u>If you don't have a vision, then it's not possible to set proper goals because you will have no idea where you're going.</u>

In Strong's Concordance, the word *perish* is the Hebrew word *para* (H6944) and it means:

**"to let go, let loose, ignore, let alone."**

According to the Strong's Concordance the Hebrew word for *law* is the word *towrah* (H8451) which means:

**"law, direction, instruction."**

Now let's go a little further. According to Strong's Concordance *happy* is the Hebrew word *esher* (H835) and it means:

**"happiness, blessedness."**

In fact, the word *esher* is in the Hebrew Concordance of the King James Bible a total of 45 times in 42 verses. And 27 of those times the word is translated as *blessed.*

If you don't have a vision, somewhere you've lost or are ignoring the revelatory insight God is trying to give you. Adhering to His instructions for the divine vision for your life ... will make you happy and blessed.

Your vision is a revelatory directive from God, and if you want to be happy and blessed ... then you need to find it and walk in it.

If you don't know what your vision is or if you have one but are unsure of what to do with it, <u>God has given me seven vision keys for you to maximize your kingdom effectiveness.</u>

## First, how do you see yourself?

Abraham was not seeing himself the way God saw him. So, the first thing God did was change his name from Abram to

Abraham because Abraham means "father of many nations." **Abraham "saw" himself as "childless" but God had a different vision of Abraham's future.**

Every time someone called to Abraham, they were speaking or confessing him to be a father of many nations.

Genesis 15:2 shows that Abraham allowed unbelief to over-whelm and control his imagination.

> "... Lord God, what wilt thou give me, seeing I go childless?"

Then, God did a second thing to help Abraham "see" himself as a part of the vision God had given him.

In Genesis 15:5-6 God called Abraham out of his tent so he could visualize the stars in the skies as his descendants.

Everything began to change once Abraham began to "see" himself in the vision God had given him ... as the father of many nations.

If your goal is to become debt free and walk in God's abundant provision, then you need to "see yourself" as God sees you ... above and not beneath ... the head and not the tail ... debt free and having more than enough.

## Second, your vision must be specific.

Joshua 1:4 states:

> "From the wilderness ... even unto the great river Euphrates, all the land ... shall be your coast."

Notice that God was very specific about the vision He gave

His people. He didn't say "... just go and pick out some piece of land somewhere." He had a choice, handpicked piece of real estate in mind for them, and He told them its specific boundaries.

It's part of God's divine nature to be specific about visions. Remember, it's the devil's plan for people to be stuck living day to day without direction or purpose in their lives.

Please get this down in your spirit: **Unless you are specific about your vision, you will never bring forth God's best for your life**.

Psalm 25:12 in The Living Bible tells us:

*"Where is the man who fears the Lord? God will teach him how to choose the best."*

For instance, it's not enough to say that I want a raise ... you've got to get specific about the amount.

Our God ... is a God of specificity.

## Third, you must write down your vision.

For the past few days God has been repeating the words of Habakkuk 2:2 in my spirit ... and now I know why. He wants me to share them with you to impact your future.

In fact, as I was praying about what scripture to use in this teaching ... Habakkuk 2:2 came clearly into my mind. It's the scripture the Lord gave me for you.

*"And the Lord ... said, Write the vision, and make it plain ... that he may run that readeth it. For the vision ... shall speak ... it will surely come, it will not tarry."*

The Contemporary English Version says:

> "Then the LORD told me: 'I will give you my message in the form of a vision. **_Write it clearly enough to be read at a glance_**.' "

Your vision must be written down <u>very clearly</u>. If you are asking yourself what your vision should be, then ask yourself this: What lives in my heart? Whatever you love God has placed in your heart for a reason. Keep reviewing your vision until you have made it as clear and precise as you can.

## Fourth, you must fully realize that God will help you win every battle the devil brings against the fulfillment of His vision for you.

Acts 5:39 says:

> "But if it be of God, ye cannot overthrow it; lest haply ye be found even to fight against God."

I love the Amplified translation of that verse.

> "But if it is of God, you will not be able to stop or overthrow or destroy them; you might even be found fighting against God!"

If you will walk according to God's vision for your life, you will never have to face defeat again. Writing the vision will loose the power of heaven on your behalf.

Remember this, **you're not fighting against the devil … instead the devil is fighting against you.** He doesn't want your God-given purpose to succeed. But he can easily be overcome because he cannot stand against the Word of God.

**God will help you win every battle.** Just remember as it says in 2 Chronicles 20:15: *"... the battle is not yours ... it's the Lord's."*

## Fifth, you must do it TODAY!

Now is the time ... this is the day for you to write your vision. It's your time to define your destiny ... it's your day to take hold of your future and unleash all the potential that God has placed in you.

**It's time to stop making excuses and make it happen.**

Now I'm going to give you a scripture that will make you shout "Shandi!"

Exodus 13:3 in the Message Bible says:

> *"Moses said to the people, 'Always remember this day. This is the day when you came out of Egypt from a house of slavery. God brought you out of here with a powerful hand. Don't eat any raised bread.'"*

This is the day ... that you purpose in your heart to come out of Egypt (financial bondage and debt) and move into God's revelatory instructions for your finances.

I will never tell you that you can be debt free in a day ... but I will tell you there is coming a day when you will know that you're going to be debt free ... and this is that day.

## Sixth, regularly review your progress in the manifestation of God's given focus for your life.

I encourage you to write clearly and specifically your vision for the upcoming year and review it on a regular basis. Do this in each of the six major areas of your life: **spiritual, physical, mental, social, financial** and **family**. Write the vision and make it plain.

Psalm 18:20 in the Message Bible says:

> *"God made my life complete when I placed all the pieces before him. When I got my act together, he gave me a fresh start. Now I'm alert to God's ways; I don't take God for granted. Every day I **review** the ways he works; I try not to miss a trick. I feel put back together, and I'm watching my step. God rewrote the text of my life when I opened the book of my heart to his eyes."*

## Seventh, keep a journal or Word document on your progress.

This effective visual will be of immeasurable assistance to you.

You must testify of God's revelatory instructions and the manifestation of all the things that He has stirred in your spirit and life.

The key to you establishing your victory and protecting you against every attack of the enemy is found in Revelation 12:11:

> *"And they overcame him by the blood of the Lamb, and by the word of their testimony; and they loved not their lives unto the death."*

Every great leader ... should have a written record and/or testimony of what they've been able to accomplish ... so it will benefit future generations.

Senator Robert Kennedy once said:

> *"Some men see things as they are and say why. I dream things that never were and say why not."*

Sadly, over the years, I've talked with many people who, with great enthusiasm, told me about their dreams filled with ambitious plans ... yet nothing ever happened.

It's one thing to dream ... and dream we must ... but it's totally another thing to make your dreams come true. Just talking about something isn't going to make it happen. We must arise and do something about it.

There comes a point when you have to stop talking ... and even quit praying ... and just be about what God has planned for you.

Exodus 14:15 in The Living Bible says:

> *"Then the Lord said to Moses, 'Quit praying and get the people moving! Forward, march!' "*

# 5 – Fold Leadership

## Invite Harold Herring to speak at your church, event, or rally.

Would you like to invite Harold to be a guest speaker at your church, event, or rally? Just send an email to:

**booking@haroldherring.com**

**or call 1-800-583-2963**

With a mix of humor, practical strategies, and Biblical insight Harold will inspire, encourage, and prepare you to change your financial destiny and set you on the path to not only set you free from debt but keep you free of debt and living the debt free life God has called you to.

Keep Thinking Rich Thoughts,

*Harold Herring*

# Join me each week!

This free email is something no one should be without. I guarantee you will be glad you signed up.

*Harold Herring*

# RichThoughts Weekly Email

### Weekly Videos

### Practical Strategies

### Biblical Insights

### Thought Provoking Humor

These are just a few of the things you are missing if you're not signed up for the RichThoughts Weekly Email.

To sign up visit:
**www.RichThoughts.org**
and get ready to be inspired, encouraged, and entertained.